The Silent Partner

The Nicholas Roerich Poetry Prize is an annual
first-book competition sponsored by the
Nicholas Roerich Museum in New York City.

1988

The Volcano Inside by David Dooley

1989

Without Asking by Jane Ransom

1990

Death, But at a Good Price by Chris Semansky

1991 CO-WINNERS

The Buried Houses by David Mason

Desire's Door by Lee McCarthy

1992

30 Miles from J-Town by Amy Uyematsu

1993

House Without a Dreamer by Andrea Hollander Budy

1994

Counterpoint by David Alpaugh

Each volume of the Nicholas Roerich Poetry Prize
Library is in print and available from:

Story Line Press
Three Oaks Farm
Brownsville, OR 97327

The Silent Partner

Greg Williamson

Story Line Press / *1995*

Published by Story Line Press, Inc., Three Oaks Farm, Brownsville, OR 97327

This publication was made possible thanks in part to the generous support of the Nicholas Roerich Museum, the Andrew W. Mellon Foundation, and our individual contributors.

Library of Congress Cataloging-in-Publication Data

Williamson, Greg, 1964–
      The silent partner / Greg Williamson.
         p. cm.
      ISBN 1-885266-11-1
      I. Title.
   PS3573.I456273S55   1995
   811'.54—dc20   95-15725
                                                      CIP

For my family and for Karen

The Silent Partner

I

II

I

Drawing Hands

Way on back in the reign of Mrs. Duke
All of the small subjects went in fear
Of her, her stormy eyes, her thunderhead
Of hair. Daily on the wall's clean slate,
She wrote the language he would learn to live
With: words and rules and examples of the rules
Whereby nouns adverbly verb their objects,
So that he might call things as he saw them.

There in the classroom, under a cloud of chalk,
How smoothly his attention used to glide
To the glass, to water braided on the glass,
Clearly clear, and standing still as it ran
Away, and deeper into the misted day
Where fields began dissolving into felt
And a stonefaced house reflected on the street.
Then the ruler would crack across his hand.

That boy lived my life ago, and whether
I leave him soloing at his desk today
Under the unbroken rules of Mrs. Duke
Or walking home through the mystifying day,
He finds his winding way back here somehow,
Where I sit high in the head of the house,
Writing and rewriting him, and watching the rain,
Which is what I came in out of for.

Figures of Speech

Under a tree across the grassy reach
Sat men and women signing each to each.

Their passionate hands maneuvered like wild birds,
Embellishing the air with figured speech
Whose meanings I could not put into words,

As if their flying fingers spoke in tongues.
Where breezes in a tree are never heard
And the songs of birds are silently unsung,

The language must be foreign as the land.
Perhaps, as painters hear the waves among
The grass with aural eyes, they understand

The frequencies of light and shade and stone
In idioms they've written out by hand,
Conversing with the world by picturephone.

Then, by degrees, across the silent lawn,
In tree trunk bass and gravel baritone
And the shook maraca of the sunlit frond,

I thought I saw the day begin to speak,
Though what it had to say I can't repeat.

Eye Strain

Toeing the mark, with the big block E charted
across the room—the moment the doctor said
"Read this line" and he replied "What line?"

it was clear that what he needed now
was glasses and that all those times he thought
he couldn't believe his eyes, he couldn't. How long,

he asked himself, had he been seeing wrong
the world? How long hoodwinked? He'd crossed a line
somewhere along the gradient to blindness,

as if he'd sat the hundred years behind
a dormer as its house declined to ruin,
and watched the garden through the warping glass

become a smear of blooms and ravelled stems.
If the signatures in things were forgeries,
how much had he misread, the way his brother,

colorblind and playing in the sprinkler's
rainbow, had learned the common names for his
uncommon spectrum? In the yard beyond

the window, no telling what mysteries were held:
a lost shoe lolling its tongue, a damp white note,
an upturned stone? He wouldn't know what things

he didn't see, but what he freshly saw
was a whole world of blurry lines: the mullion
itself, the liquid corner of a house

across the lawn, and the sidewalk's cirrus edge
where it ran beside the house and disappeared
between the smudges of rose and a mist of green.

Story and Song

Now going nowhere and already late,
Caught in traffic, he scanned the radio
And suddenly recalled the seventy-eight
A string band had recorded long ago,
His first record, won at a county fair
And squeaking on the magical machine
Whose stylus tracked as if downhill along
The coded grooves in which he used to stare
At moving stillness, enchanted that between
The vinyl and the diamond was a song.

And staring he saw such imaginings,
As if the very kitchen came alive.
With washboard, bottles, jug and brassy strings,
They made a music out of daily life
From which the music may have been escape.
On a ruined porch they gathered in a ring,
The banjoist sidesaddle on the rail.
The mountain wore its shadow like a cape,
And a black path meandered to a spring
That disappeared in laurel below the trail.

The ballad's girl had gone to wash her hair
And wandered the stream too far into a grove
Of ordinary trees, from which no prayer
Could save her. By afternoon the boy in love
Had found her yellow bonnet where it lay
And followed down the unforgiving hill.
He is the hoot owl asking who and why.
She is the sound of water running away.

As long as the song is sung they wander still
Confounded by the woods, in common time.

The band by now must be disbanded, wracked
By drink or age and gone around the bend.
He'd played their song until the tenor cracked,
The banjo blurred and words came to an end
One afternoon where the boy and girl remained
Apart, except in dreams beyond the dream.
With the signal he moved on, the music hushed.
The hard and clamorous world was little changed,
But he recalled the singing of a stream
And that it wore a diamond down to dust.

Fields of Vision

When he found a camera buried among his socks,
  A secret present from his aunt,
  The boy endeavored to transplant
The whole of his journey to that window box,

To catch the wind that riffled through the wheat
  And stroked the beards of barleycorn
  And, like a flock not quite airborne,
Taxied the millpond on a million feet.

The moving scenery fled before his eyes
  As neither wheels nor weather stopped,
  But the window of his camera cropped
The panoramic farmlands down to size.

Up in his room, when the photos were returned,
  He looked into the faces of the days.
  Deep in the grain and acred haze
The kernel of half-truth could be discerned:

He recognized the places and the names,
  And yet the quick, familiar range
  Had grown composed, remote and strange,
And the wind blew beyond the shuttered frames.

But matting both the graces and the gaffes,
  Although the boy could not see why
  The world he pictured made him cry,
He harvested his crop of photographs.

Junkyard

Where the tall towers of the city rise
Deep in the distance across a river bend,
The fading traces of a gravel drive
Run off the county highway through a field
Of all the usual grasses to the banks,
Where hidden in Queen Anne's lace and goldenrod
A junkyard lies at the end of the road, unused
And gone to grass in the shadow of the city.

Or else it is the shadow of the city,
Whose time has come and will not come again,
Except for what we make of it from these
Twice ruined ruins. Down in the dumps of Troy
Cracked urns and ornate scraps of fired clay
And broken bits in turn reflected Troy
Beyond the walls, and testify that they
Were crafty artisans and horsemen and
Indeed they were beseiged for many years.

Down here blue flies and butterflies and bees,
The water's running thump against its banks,
The sunlight glimmering in shattered glass
As the yard explodes with crickets every step,
All deepen the stillness of a burned-out stove,
Radiators, a listing water heater.
(In a cold world they were a people who
Had trouble keeping warm.) And one sees tires
And tractors here, a dozen diesel drums,
A concrete mixer, bales of barbed wire,

Blank televisions, box springs, a commode.
(They farmed and built and played. They carried on.)

But mostly what one notices are cars.
Flamboyant chrome, the engines and the fins,
The size and extra racks say much about
The people who possessed them, but in the names
We see the way they must have seen themselves:
DeSoto Coronado, Phoenix, Bel Air,
Roadmaster, Nomad Wagon, Maverick,
Rambler, Galaxy, and Eldorado.
(They yearned for going more than getting there.)

These are the easy emblems of our race:
Of fire and forge and factory, of long
Assembly lines, emblems of oil and speed,
Of city and suburb and the rush to work,
Of traffic jams and of the wanderlust
We've always loved about ourselves. (They were
Romantic, reckless, migratory people.)

Under the sun in the lively yard, how slowly
Smolders the inexorable decay.
The grills grin on insanely with chrome teeth.
Hoods gape. There is no light in the deadman stare
Of headlights, no faces in the empty mirrors,
Where bonelike struts and pipes are scattered among
The skeletons of mice and the spent shells
Of cicadas. A brittle snakeskin suns itself

On a rock, and one thinks of all the absent souls
Who wore their bodies out.

                              No doubt there was
Great sadness in these wrecks, happiness too.
Possibly because I am young, I think
Of them as young, the kids of another time
Who turned the keys and brought the behemoths
To life, who cruised the parties and midnight roads
And went to work and drove away to school.
Despite the somberness of smashed front ends,
Cracked windshields and a bullet-riddled door,
How dated and naive those children seem,
Behind the wheel or taken for a ride,
Now that ivy has climbed in the back seats
And water stagnates in the pickup beds
Where, once, in parking lots or country roads
Our discontinued parents ground their gears.

The great chimneys burn across the river.
Whatever we are, we will become whatever
Is said about us. That goes without saying,
Although one could be wrong about a place
Where wind in dry grass sounds like rain. Time comes
To go. And I leave under the stewardship
Of crickets and flies and pollinating bees
The reclamation project of the weeds.

The Carpenters

Still half-asleep and often still half-drunk,
They bitch about their wives and trucks and work.
The Skil saws lurch. A hammer hits a thumb
Or bangs a nail over or splits the wood
At a crucial joint, which anyway was out
Of square or measured wrong; then bending down
To pull the thing, his butt peeps out above
His pants. Mostly that's how things get done.

But certain afternoons, with men arrayed
Around the frame, the sun appears to gleam
In sawdust winnowing behind the blade
And catch the hammer cocked above a beam
In a still life of the legendary glamour
Of craft and craftmanship the mind is given
Long since and far away, where the poised hammer
Doesn't fall, and not a nail gets driven.

Walter Parmer

I

How many children must have come to pass
Beyond that door and join the long sojourn
When school bells rang the students into class

To see the world from inside out and learn
To read the words and say the magic spells
That might unlock the door for their return?

Here first they faced the guarded citadels
Of otherness, and faced the windowpane
With all it had to show them of themselves,

Strange and familiar in the standing rain,
And caught the primer's hint of mystery
When early words took shape and Jack saw Jane

And Jane looked back, as neither one would be
The same for that. But when the bell would ring
For recess, playing was its own grand prix:

The mystifying movement of the swing,
The lofty goals and races to the fence,
And basketballs more real than anything.

II

Out there the wintry playground seemed immense,
Their kitty of little words too small and blind
To make the world of sight and sound make sense,

Where at day's end one child was kept behind
To clap the powdery lessons back to chalk,
Which lingered in the wind and on the mind.

In spring they made the graduated walk
Through the elementary door and filed away,
Learning to leave as they had learned to talk.

That was the way it was, until one May
Officials put a padlock on the door
And called a final summer holiday.

In the blank stare those empty windows wore,
How lushly did the stillness seem to flower
Across a schoolyard where the neighbors swore,

Although the hands sat still in their clock tower
And the schoolhouse stood in silence, out of time,
They heard the class bells ringing on the hour.

III

On the first warm Saturday past wintertime
And through the bonfire summer into fall,
The ragweed on the fence begins to climb,

And the old boys man the court for basketball.
They pivot, dribble, juke, and sweat all day
Because they love that moment when the ball

Hangs in an arcing, flawless fadeaway
Or hits a backdoor cutter in the hands,
Some small extemporaneous display

Of grace, though every player understands
That timing falters: the jumpshot that almost
Fell in falls off, a pass skips out of bounds.

The losers leave the court; that is the cost
Of losing where a challenger appears
And winners keep on winning till they've lost.

They play a game they've played for thirty years,
Though rosters fluctuate with crossed-out names
And days turn into seasons and careers.

IV

The players were the first to notice flames
When Parmer burned. They phoned in their report
And in the sun resumed their heated games.

Along the split rail fence beyond the court,
The neighbors reconvened, whose early laughter
Welled up in tears to see the flames cavort

Across the ridge and tightrope every rafter,
To hear the building pop as windows broke,
While newsmen asked their thoughts about disaster.

The men and women cried and vaguely spoke
Of teachers, friends, and unresolved desire
That seemed just then were going up in smoke.

The rolling cameras showed the school expire
And showed the boys' apparent unconcern
As small-time Neros, backlit by a fire,

Playing along, performing in their turn,
While embers fell like autumn, red and gold,
Because the game goes on though buildings burn.

V

After a long debate, the school board sold
The brick for salvage and bulldozed the paved
Piazza where the students had enrolled.

In a vacant quarter of the yard they saved
Only the stone abutments and the arch,
Above which "Walter Parmer" was engraved.

Where parents walked a path around the park
And children rode the swings and players played,
A high school couple rolls up after dark,

Fondling through an FM serenade,
Learning another tongue and reading love
On lips that taste like gin and lemonade.

In window fog they write their names above
A steamy heart of hot and vagabond
Devotions, while that distant figure of

An oracle seems ready to respond
With secret wisdom, waiting on a word,
Opening out to nowhere but beyond.

VI

Back on the court the clatter of voices blurred
And blew away. A young man stands before
That arch, a ball on his hip. Something stirred,

He thinks, like shoes scuffing a wooden floor.
And then a chalk stick squeaks across clean slate,
Like a dry hinge turning. Down the hall a door

Is opening on a room where a classmate
Is looking at a warping windowpane,
Whose standing streams appear to corrugate

Both field and glass, and looking through the rain
He dreams a summer day and takes good aim
To see the ball go in again and again.

Then voices call the fellow to his game.
The schoolhouse vanishes. His team is on,
And he turns back to leave the way he came.

Only the arch remains, something like dawn,
An empty doorway on the open grass,
Standing for going, as well as having gone.

Outbound

*We live life forwards and think
about it backwards.*

Howard Nemerov

We passengers ride backward on the train
And train our eyes on what has passed us by.
    A cobalt blur composes
    Into a woman picking roses,
Who is already fading in the pane
As in the failing hindsight of the eye.

A line of oaks comes into focus, fades,
Supplanted by the double-dagger poles
    Of power companies,
    Footnotes that redefine the trees.
An asterisk in glass, then window shades,
Graffiti, billboards, tattered banderoles

Of southbound birds. . . . Whatever comes to view
Corrects the view, but never will explain
    The random next event
    Or anything but where we went,
Where long ago a woman wearing blue
Began forgetting someone on a train.

Chant Royal

One of modern architecture's greatest failings has been its lack of interest in the relationship of the building to the sky. One doubts that a poem was ever written to a flat-roofed building silhouetted against the setting sun.

Paul Randolph

Imagine the architect's early discontent
With wooden blocks or musty counterpane
Draping across the table like a tent,
Already found too flimsy and mundane
For a girl who dreamed of spires and tower clocks,
Looking across the domed and pitched terrain
Of roofs. And now to stand in a great glass building
And stare down on the glistening gridlocks
And contemplate the job she's just begun:
To diagram another flat-roofed building
Silhouetted against the setting sun.

Late nights deciphering each document,
Learning the books, the styles, the fine arcane
Refinements of the guild; what keen torment
To look across the panoramic chain
Of burger shops, the whitebread Bun-in-a-Box,
Closed circuit malls and movieplex, domain
Of the hopelessly bored, who cruise a tinsel building
As in some sleek florescent Skinner box
Of Muzak, mirrors, and shiny three-for-one
Diamelle displays in a flat-roofed building
Silhouetted against the setting sun.

She'd seen a couple in one of those cement
And I-beam towers, wrapped in cellophane
To look like televisions, where the vent

Exhales a sibilant, chalky Novocain
To feed the plastic ferns and gleaming locks
Of laquered hair. She had seen their smiles drain
Like Pepsi, as they mounted a desk, building
A rhythm: her legs in the air, he stood in his socks.
They banged and sobbed and screamed for all or none,
Fucking for dear life in a flat-roofed building
Silhouetted against the setting sun.

The gimcrack sprawls across the continent:
Doomed kitchenettes in simulated grain,
The paste and paper condos made to rent,
In which each standard untrimmed windowpane
Is rattling and all the plumbing knocks—
Threatening to melt with the first good rain,
Like giant tracts of sugar cubes they're building.
But down below, somehow, on streets and docks
The Fades and Crew Cuts get the workdays done,
Like some austere and silent flat-roofed building
Silhouetted against the setting sun.

She imagines that anonymous Resident
Picking up his mail, the brood of inane
Blow-ins that flutter from a supplement,
A hardware owner putting on the chain
At a block and panel storage room, and flocks
Of dusky birds at windbreaks on the plain
Where cattle nose away and storms are building.
She thinks of nightshift boys who check the stocks

And of putting up her feet on an empty tun
On the terrace of her sublet flat-roofed building
Silhouetted against the setting sun.

Out at the county line, the sun is gilding
The causeway, where a shed of cinderblocks
Houses the antiquated pumps that run,
And go on running, in a flat-roofed building
Silhouetted against the setting sun.

Nature Poem

*When a Gunnison's [prairie dog] sees a person and gives
an alarm, it doesn't simply say, "Predator!" It actually says, for
example, "Tall dark thin man!" With humans, they will scurry
into their burrows, then pop their heads back out to watch.*

The Baltimore Sun

For so long nature never said a word.
Whenever storms harangued or seas would rage,
Whenever thrush or skylark would be heard
To warn, or trees to whisper in the winds,
We knew that we were standing just offstage,
Throwing our voices, speaking their many minds.

But if they could speak, we had speculated,
They'd love us, care for us, or be profound
At least in their uncaring; so we waited,
Leaving them speechless even as we sought
To speak some sentence into every sound.
That was the nature of the world we thought.

Now we have intercepted on the prairie
Gunnison's sentries calling to the clan,
And finally cracked the code: "Sh! Be wary!
Go to your homes.
Tall dark thin man
This way comes."

Bradley Woodhouse

The squirrels got in the attic room
One day, where Bradley Woodhouse read
His books and wrote and laid his head.
The envoys came across a limb
To reconnoiter empty space
Inside the walls and sloping roof.
And Bradley Woodhouse found it cute,
At first, and inspirational
To have the natural world so near
At hand and chattering to him.

The cocker spaniel, though, was not
Amused and gnashed her teeth and chased
Her hidden demons through the room.

Bradley Woodhouse listened hard
And tried to write what things he heard,
As if he thought some natural
Divinity would speak itself
Into the musings of his soul.
The squirrels were reluctant, though,
To be turned into metaphors
Or leave their riddles plainly said.
Their chattering might rise to screams
Or might grow sinisterly still
And let a tentative repose
Diffuse about the frazzled house,
Then burst into a crazy laugh.
And Bardley Wordhound found his heart

Grown jumpy to anticipate
The next mad dash across the beams
Or wrestling match inside the wall.

The days wore on. And then the dog
Was howling at the closet door
Where Beardsley Workhorse heard a troupe
Of acrobatic, flying squirrels
Performing on the clothes trapeze.
And peeking with his flash he found
The interlopers in his shoes
And in the pockets of his shirts,
Wearing his clothes, eating his belts,
And ogling, he thought, a coupled pair
That turned up in an upturned hat.

They had begun to colonize.
The wads of paper that he stuffed
Along their trading routes became
Upholstery. They stole his socks.
They urinated on his traps.
All day they chattered in his ears;
All night they scampered overhead.
The plaster sifted in his eyes
That stared a dangerous ceiling down,
And acorns rolled around the floor.

Composing at his wooden desk,
Whenever Batty Weirdout cracked
His nervous knuckles, cracked a nut

And rooted in the dusty floor,
Which buckled as the saplings grew
To roomy oaks, whose canopy
Spread darkly through the shady air.
The pages of his journal turned
Between his fingers into leaves,
Twittering with flocks of birds.
Whenever he put stick to leaf,
They cawed and cackled in his head.

Unwalked, unfed, the spaniel howled
And marked frenetically the trees,
Whose trunks had thickened with the rings
Of his unanswered telephone.
And Birdy Wordy was afraid.
The lamp shade's golden owlish eyes
Hunted the corners of the room,
And when it turned its terrible head
The dust mice ran beneath the bed.
Yellow leaves fluttered on his desk,
And shadows prowled around his feet.
Into his room the curtains blew
And blustered in his stormy room
Like clouds which rained on him cold sweat,
Sweet clouds which colded on him rain.

And Bobbily Wobbily went outside
One day and squatted in a tree.
The murderous birds grew quiet then.
The neighbors asked him to get down.

The squirrels watching from the sill
Said, "Now we've got him where we want."
But Boogily Woogily never heard
A word that anybody said,
Above the chatter in his squirrelly head.

You Are Here

The snowy voices in my head debate
    About the radio
And where I am along the interstate
And after so much coffee, can I wait?
    I go until I have to go.

Beside the glowing Coffeemax machine
    A roadmap on the door
Says, "You are here": beside a dank latrine
At a vacant rest stop set somewhere between
    What lies behind me and before.

To be some where at all is some relief.
    The night is desolate and deep,
Where midnight preachers question my belief
And songmen modulate through love to grief
    To make the very headlights weep.

I cannot solve the theologian's quiz
    Nor read the stars to steer,
But when my sleepy self asks where he is,
Between the coffee and another whiz,
    I tell him, "Quiet. You are here."

Italics, Mine

Hello, up there. Thank God you happened by.
   I'm touched. I've been beneath the covers
   For so long now the light is stark,
Where honestly I thought that I might lie
   Alone forever in the dark,
      And this is a place for lovers.

By night I dreamed about the day you looked
   And read my thoughts and would agree
   To spend some time with me, and talk.
Since all the flights to Paris have been booked,
   Perhaps you'd settle for a walk
      To see what we shall see.

You see that oak leaf there? I always sense
   A kinship with the leaves. To me
   Each one portrays a little oak,
A fragile replica of an immense
   Black oak, itself a lush, baroque,
      Green forest of a tree.

And at the shore let's walk the water line,
   The ocean's flexing, outermost
   Advance, where the seawater laps
A sandy beach, plotting a jagged line
   Whose every subdivision maps
      A continental coast.

Or looking backward toward the mountain range,
   We see the ridge line's collarbone,

Comprising summit and ravine,
And holding up a rock we find a strange,
Profound affinity between
The mountains and the stone.

If I seem to be beginning to repeat
Myself, it is because the world
Repeats itself in hidden laws
Whose figurings and fractals the exegete
Tries to articulate because
In the beginning was the word.

As with the sense of humor in a laugh,
In every word a poem survives,
Abundantly rich in ways and means
To build the sentence and the paragraph,
The rise and fall of little scenes,
The stories of our lives.

The coming home of walks and talks and stories
Discloses what we came to know,
Where the changing fortunes of a day
Become a lifetime's sadnesses and glories,
A stranger's face to which we say,
As to the mirror, "Hello."

Hello. I hope you pardon my conceits,
But I have dreamed on my nightstands
From all these little rooms to build
A home where we might lie between the sheets,

And I declare myself fulfilled
When I am in your hands.

But this has all been talk, I know, and I
Can tell you are about to turn
And go your way, while I repair
To darkness and a dateless night. Goodbye.
I will be saying a silent prayer
That one day you return.

The River-Merchant's Wife: A Letter

Before I grew my bangs, Lisa and me
Were smoking in the Krystal parking lot,
And you and Mike drove by in The Grey Ghost.
You had just got your earring then, remember?
"How 'bout a ride?" you said, and I said,
"If you're driving." I barely had my boobs,
But we ran all the stop signs to the park.
God, I was so wet, but I wouldn't.
Every time we moved, you knocked the horn.
I think about that now.

How long? In Cleveland is it cold?
I keep the floodlights on all night.
When I pull in the driveway from the shop,
Charlie sits at the fence. He looks so sad.

I've mowed four times since you've been gone.
And now the yard's knee-deep in maple leaves.
They seem more red this year.
Mike called. He had some tickets for the game.
Everybody misses you, you know. Already
The air smells cold, it smells like football;
And the school bus comes by every morning.
That was so long ago.
Please call me soon.
Please tell me when you're coming home.
        I bought some lingerie.

Belvedere Marittimo

My dear, you would not believe the weather here.
The postcard doesn't do it justice, nor
Can I. But notice how the sun's great mint
Is stamping silver coins upon the sea,
Scooning away whole treasuries of change
On pelicans, bikinis, the lacy flounce
Of surf. And notice, too, in the flowerbed
How lady-slippers and narcissi blush
Beside the bedsheets luffing on a line,
And how the watercolor limes and pinks
Of the little summer cottages appear
To be the very picture of repose.

For seven days I've looked out of my room
On none of this. A bankrupt, dishrag sky
Wrings out a steady mizzle on the beach,
An indigent hachure which drains away
The washes of pastel to shades of grey
As bleary, wet and untranslatable
As every sodden page of *il giornale*.
Sinister, small black birds clothespin the line.
"The piers are pummelled by the waves." I write,
Perhaps, to weather this foul weather, dear.
The rain runs down the glass. Wish you were here.

On the International Date Line

I

In far Japan, Land of the Rising Sun,
The rising yen, the businesspeople wait
Even before the new day has begun,

Crowded against an airport lounge's gate,
To taste the newest Beaujolais Nouveau,
Which is not sold before a certain date,

Arriving in their archipelago
Before the world has finished off the last
Of yesterday or yesterday's Bordeaux.

It is a perfect present from the past:
To be the first to celebrate the flash
When sunlight catches on some mizzenmast

And rises like a phoenix from the ash
Of sunset, night, and dark uncertainty;
To be on the cusp where all the tenses clash,

Where spirits of the Old World oversee,
Out of the grave, the grape, the gravest night,
The future of the countries oversea.

II

Midway in the Pacific, our acolyte
Lights out across the Date Line heading west,
Where time unravels and the days rewrite,

As though upon a scrolling palimpsest,
Recycled daily like the *The Daily Globe*,
The subplots of our interweaving geste

With a cast of billions and a vast wardrobe.
If we could straddle that imagined fence
Between the dates of our diurnal strobe,

If briefly we could leave the present tense,
Where all our flawed performances are live,
And read the past's account of our expense,

Recast a scene, rewrite the narrative,
If we could read the stage directions for
Some future act, to find where we arrive....

But no. And you have heard this all before.
We cannot see what sights we will have seen,
And all we ever saw is nevermore.

III

The International Date Line lies between
Two continents, in the middle of the sea.
As with the dark stage following a scene

Or the white space which divides an elegy,
One cannot say just when the days exhume
Themselves, deep in that darkness, quietly.

But when the lights go up and words resume,
The new world seems, itself, a world apart
And written in a novel nom de plume,

Except this tragic drama is not art,
With its rehearsals and its rubber swords.
Each actor gets one reading of his part

And opening night, alone, to tread the boards.
We pay in time for the little time we borrow,
And lull ourselves to sleep by looking towards

Tomorrow and tomorrow and tomorrow,
The bedside words of all our yesterdays,
A sorry promise promising more sorrow.

IV

The dawn is but a thin, prevailing haze
Of pencillings and phosphors which suffuse
The night before it slinks toward alleyways,

Clandestine coves. The disembodied blues
And purples, shadowy reminders, tend
The fishing boats and bays as ghostly crews.

The sins and amends of night and day amend
Each other. It is impossible to say
The darknesses of night entirely end.

The Japanese look out across the bay
For the frontispiece of day's new folio.
In suits and socks, making a grand display

Of pouring out the Beaujolais Nouveau,
They sing and slap their backs, but their eyes shine
With all the gay solemnity we know

When New Year's Eve is singing "Auld Lang Syne."
They weep for all that is and is not done,
And raise their slender glasses to the wine.

Smoke Signals

The slender, pencilled lines
Of smoke drift from the chimneys to the wind
And, drafting on the sky, belly and bend
Like alphabetic signs,

As if some ghostwriter scripts
In runes of foreign language manuals,
Or the bearded, ornamental uncials
Of ancient manuscripts,

The legend of our lives
Which nobody can read except to note
The vagrant wind erases what it wrote
Before a word survives.

One thing we do not doubt,
The world seems riddled with these loops and shanks
Enciphering the sky, filling the blanks,
Spelling the whole thing out.

The Man in the Window

At night in lighted rooms, who has not seen
      His dark reflection in the glass,
            His countenence impose
            On the cold rains and snows
      That fall in the world beyond the glass,
As if his figure figured in that scene?

            On the bus I used to ride
      To school, I watched my image fly
Across the fixed addresses as they flew
Across the window I was looking through,
      Where he was passed or passing by
            The permanent outside.

Looking out, I have seen him looking in
      At the schoolboy suddenly alone,
            The man across the mall
            Or far end of the hall,
      The boyfriend on the telephone,
The stranger playing poker where I'd been.

            Somehow I cannot say
      Just how the haunting haunted eyes
Have seemed to dream disparate worlds together:
I am projecting him on rainy weather,
      But looking back in my disguise
            He's watching what I say.

Oh I know it's fanciness—the interface
    Shows just the figure I expect,
        No ghost, no shadowy Cain,
        But rather me again
    Learning the ins and outs—except
All night the dog's been snarling at that face.

II

The Counterfeiter

When he was starting out, still green,
He used to make a signature mistake
So that his hidden talent could be seen,
Reversing the flag above the White House roof.
It made him feel ingenious and aloof
To signify his forgeries as fake.

He always liked his jokes, but they are private.
Sometimes, when he is pressed about his trade,
He answers with a shrug, "I draw a profit"
Or "I trust in God." Nobody ever laughs.
In the den, above two ebony giraffes,
Hangs the first dollar that he ever made.

But making money is an enterprise
Of tedious, grave concerns. To reproduce
These symboled reproductions, his hands and eyes
Must settle on what others merely see,
The couples, columns and the Model T,
And all the framework, intricate, abstruse,

And difficult to copy by design,
With fine acanthuses and cycloid nets.
He must account for every tiny line
To duplicate the sad and distant stare
Beneath the breaking waves of Jackson's hair,
If he would tender these to pay his debts.

He has invested his adult career
In being perfect when he goes to press,
An artistry both humble and severe.
Down at the basement desk, long hours pass
With a burin and a magnifying glass.
No one suspects his notable success.

He profits by his anonymity,
But deep regret competes with honest pride:
To labor toward complete obscurity
And treasure a craft that will efface his will,
Render his name unknown and all his skill
Unrecognized, long after he has died.

In the Shield of Athena

As people watch eclipses in a pail
Or see the sun reveal itself a star
In ponds and windowpanes, drawn down to scale,
When Perseus drew out his scimitar

To slay Medusa and assure his fame,
He held the stony gaze that none could hold
By holding her reflection in a frame,
Then journeyed on to gardens made of gold.

Some things we cannot look at, but in stealth
We fancy grand abstractions, love and time,
(Which runs like water, circulates like wealth)
By analogue, reflection, paradigm,

And so envision shrouds of grief, the gem
Of naked beauty and the knucklebone
Of hate, such things as on the face of them
Would blind the eye or turn the heart to stone.

The Dial Tone

They had a bad connection, and the static
          Crackled like gravel drives
          Or like the sharp, erratic
Snapping of twigs among dry leaves. Their lives

Had come to this, conducted across long
          Distances. No wonder,
          She said, it all went wrong;
The heart grows firm, but it does not grow fonder,

And she who had once been so hung up on him
          Hung up on him. The phone
          Went dead, and in the dim
Quiescent living room the dial tone

Hummed in his ears that it was finally over,
          A droning vacancy
          That promised to last forever,
Like the flat, pulseless line of an E.K.G.

In which their conversation, their romance,
          This life of dull routine
          And random circumstance
Were merely interruptions on the screen.

Cross Country

From the roped margins of the steeplechase,
The crowd can read the finish in the start,
For there is one who manifests a grace
To skim the world as in a world apart.

Her spanking t-shirt animates the meadow
Under the clockwork sun, which she astounds
By drafting in the slipstream of her shadow,
Light on her feet, as he dallies on his rounds.

Sparrows are caught in stunned miscalculations.
She disappears behind a stand of trees,
And we consult our hushed imaginations,
Which conjure glimpses of Pheidippides

Racing against himself along the rim
Through olive trees and down a mountain trail
Until the distant finish finished him,
Exhausted by the bearing of his tale.

Like measured music of the steeple bells,
Like leaping salmon, or a balladeer,
Some charms dispel themselves to cast their spells,
As if. . . . But then she bursts into the clear,

And down the homestretch, far from Marathon,
She glides in the legato of good form.
At the line she stops her watch. The sun moves on.
The spirit drains out of her uniform.

Waterfall

In still transparency, the water pools
    High in a mountain stream, then spills
Over the lip and in a sheet cascades
Across the shoal, obeying hidden rules,
        So that the pleats and braids,
The feather-stitched white water, little rills
    And divots seem to ride in place
    Above the crevices and sills,
Although the water runs along the race.

What makes these rapids, this little waterfall,
    Cascading like a chandelier
Of frosted glass or like a willow tree,
Is not the water only nor the fall
        But some complicity
Of both, so that these similes appear
    Inaccurate and limited,
    Neglecting that the bed will steer
The water as the water steers the bed.

So too with language, so even with this verse.
    From a pool of syllables, words hover
With rich potential, then spill across the lip
And riffle down the page, for better or worse,
        Making their chancy trip,
Becoming sentences as they discover
    (Now flowing, now seeming to stammer)
    Their English channels, trickling over
The periodic pauses of its grammar.

Black Sand Beaches

When on the porch the conversation turned
One rainy afternoon to beaches, he learned
From his friend, the neighborhood geologist,
That in some volcanic areas exist,
Although he doubted it initially,
Beaches of black sand sloping to the sea.

The rest of the day he marvelled at that scene
As the mind went sailing on its barkentine
To the black shoulders of some Mauna Loa,
Wearing the long, white, carbonated boa
Of surf and necklaces of limpets, bleached
By sunlight on the strands where they were beached.
A woman reads the paper, as her boy
Rebuilds the lofty parapets of Troy,
A castle of basalt for the Black Knight.
A lifeguard twirls his whistle; girls in white
Bikinis amble across rich coffee grounds,
Where gulls fly low and a white retriever bounds
After a Frisbee flung into the waves—
Inverted like scratch-work, as an artist shaves
Away black ink, revealing a little school
Of clouds, swimming the smoked-glass tidal pool.

A beautiful and useless bit of knowledge.
Like most of what he knew, he must acknowledge,
It would not make him wealthier, or wise.
And yet, like Keats's watcher of the skies
Or like Miranda on the day she dwelt
In a brave new world, he felt the way he felt

Whenever he unearthed a novel word,
However trivial, arcane, absurd,
Because the name amends his universe,
Which was, for him, forever more diverse,
And might contain a marvellous black coast
Of crushed basalt. He may not ever boast
Of lounging in those strange, obsidian lands,
Sipping a drink and dawdling on the sands,
Squinting against their dark, exotic glare,
But it was good to know that they were there.

Labor Day

Truly the light is sweet and a pleasant
thing it is for the eyes to behold the sun
. . . yet let him remember the days of darkness;
for they shall be many.

Ecclesiastes 11:7-8

Eight floors below this hotel balcony
The sun conducts a light show on the pool.
Silvery lozenges ride out and burp,
Waver and double back upon themselves,
Warping like cames of mercury among
Quarrels of sky blue glass, as if this were
A latticed window, or a fluid map
Of how we try to figure out the world,
As the mind finds correspondences in things
That make the meanings we would make them mean.

These gilded filaments of light suggest
A fishnet stocking, reflective of a mild,
Unconscious lust, perhaps, for the long legs
Who sunbathe on the deck, or may suggest
As easily a stringbag that contains
The entire pool of images, or else
An undulant chain-link fence that separates
The world from us and all we think of it.

The light is sweet, of course, and people seem
Contented with their magazines and towels.
In pickets of the redwood fence, wind pipes
A cheerful ditty, a folksong for the folks
Who laugh and talk or swan dive off the board.
In the oceanic sky, an argosy
Of clouds, cartoony, animated clouds,

Famed for mercurial abilities,
Is sailing in fair weather toward a storm
Almost impossible to picture now.

This is the final day of summer. When
The sun slides down its firepole behind
The hill, the pool is closed, and everyone,
Bearing his towel and raft and radio,
Flipflops out of the gate. The lambent web,
Which played across the surface of the pool
And caught the tangled way relationships
Are made, dissolves in moods of lavender,
And water settles down into the faint,
Alluvial fans of underwater jets
And sporadic, feathered voiceprints of the breeze.

As these last wrinkles in declining light
Disperse, the water seems to disappear.
Involuntarily, the mind goes forth
Across the empty deck, trying to recall
The wayward faces of those castaways
Who seem to dwell among the silhouettes
Of chairs and closed umbrellas. Now the wind
Is like the wind that blows in trellises
Of February gardens, ropes of ships,
The iron railings of abandoned homes.
It will be a long winter, full of nights.

And now a darkening flotilla of clouds
Summons the recollection of old friends,
Lost companions, who drifted out of reach
As trading routes diverge on ancient maps.
Their ghosts survive in troubled memories
As crews of nightclouds, ominous and vague,
The spidereens upon a sea of years.

Now, far below, the sun's reflecting moon
Looks upward, small and bony, from the pool
As from a photographic negative,
Or the afterimage of a birthday flash,
Or else the bare bulb in a boarding room
Where someone, you can tell, has left in haste
With water dripping in the sink, or like
A single headlight coming around a bend
On the loneliest midnight road in Tennessee.
Search-party lights, an attic lamp in the manor
On a dead end street, a lantern swinging in
An empty shed: these hints of solitude
And panic rise on their own out of the dark,
Surface from some unfathomed reservoir,
And in the end they find their way to me.

The Mysterious Stranger

You see him everywhere, a face in the crowd.
    He lingers by your side
And stalks the shopfront windows, slightly bowed,
    Matching you stride for stride.

He lurks behind the mirrors of waiting rooms,
    Behind the marble walls
Of railway stations, banquet halls, and looms
    In the two-way mirrors of malls.

He hides in the jackets of books, in lavaliers,
    In the glossy monochrome
Of negatives, and after dark he peers
    In the windows of your home.

He knows your heart by heart, where an old disgrace
    You buried yet survives,
And secret loves reflected on your face
    In spoons and kitchen knives.

Your Doppelgänger, silent partner, laid
    Out at the bottom of lakes
And coffee cups, or loitering in the shade
    Of lamps, as long as it takes

He'll ride along in buses, welcome you
    At tinted doors, and slog
Through rainy puddles in the avenue,
    Weathering both the fog

Of light bulbs and the snow of paperweights,
    To call on you one day.
Beware of him, the stranger in town, who waits
    To give yourself away.

Narcissus . . .

Narcissus, who was never very wise,
Observed a water-spirit in a pond
And grew enamored of the comely blonde
Who matched his gaze and filled his shallow eyes.

Through all the dawns, it never dawned on him
Why such a face would shatter at a tear
And flee his touch or why the pond's veneer
Would duplicate an overhanging limb.

The spirits featured in the face of waves,
The lips of fountains or the fountainhead
Are images of us in nature's stead,
Reflecting on the way the world behaves,

And as the spring of youth matures tomorrow
To Old Man Winter and old age, we look
And look and ask the figure in the brook,
As long ago Narcissus did, "Who *are* you?"

. . . And Echo

Echo, who tricked a Queen with her replies,
Received a sentence only to respond
And gradually became a vagabond,
A voice, unable to extemporize.

Seeing Narcissus at the water's brim,
She fell in love, but when he said, "Come here,"
The timbre of the forest said, "Come, hear,"
And she became the selfless eponym

For words we put into the mouths of caves,
The teeth of canyons and the woodenhead
Ravines. Though nature's ministries seem led
By honest voices in the open naves,

Divine and inspirational and true,
The words resounding from an overlook
Are only ours, as once beside a brook,
Narcissus heard from Echo, *"Who* are *you?"*

Lost at Sea

Why in the world would Anyone set sail,
Knowing the certain, legendary fate
Of voyagers conscripted to that tale
Where Anyone upon the famed, grey slate
Of sea, anonymous and sick of home,
Will have smooth sailing, for about a week,
Learning to steer his craft across the foam
Before it begins to leak
And frightful passages destroy the sheets
And fray the lines, before the stormclouds stir
And crazy waterspouts careen like tops
To overwhelm his unimpressive feats,
As over the bones of sailors skillfuller
Than he swells of oblivion lick their chops
To dump him in the cold, intemperate drink
With nothing to grab except a floating sink,
Delirious and drifting in his cup
To a tiny island, littorally washed up?

The tale prescribes that he be in the spell
Of acrobatic Arielists who sport
Around the creek that navigates the dell
As well as in those goodly measures of port
Providentially imported by the gales,
So that he is consistently beguiled
By babbling brooks, hillocks that look like whales
And mists of all he misses, now exiled
And homesick for a past he can't reprise,
For Anyone returning would be seen

The crazed imposter of Someone lost at sea,
Where, although saucy spirits trick his eyes,
He bottles little notes from his demesne
To say he's here, wherever that may be,
Peopling his isle with eidolons,
The Idiot and *The Oddities*, his sons,
A form of recreation not to die
Dispirited and stranded, high and wry.

Annual Returns

If money grew on trees,
How happy we'd be then,
The children rolling in dough,
The fathers raking it in.

With holdings in the branches
Showing a big return,
The trees would drop a fortune,
We'd all have money to burn.

As autumn leaves, however,
We find the poor still poor.
The falling stocks in trees
Are swept away from the door.

So what became of the boy
Whom teachers had to scold,
Who stared and stared out windows
Into the lands of gold,

Where after school he spent
His lonely afternoons
And shuffled home knee-deep
In rubies and doubloons?

He listens to the leaves
That rattle in a squall,
Still dreaming of a world
That profits from the fall.

Chestnut Street

This street was named in another town
For shady characters, who stood
Their corners in the neighborhood
And grew infirm and were cut down.

American chestnut trees have come
To a dead end. The street goes on,
As if things are not wholly gone
Because their names do not succumb.

That is the hope of elegies
And memorials, that names beget
New life. Surely we won't forget
An entire family of trees,

Whose name is flowering although
The roots are buried with the men
Who did the naming way back when.
But suddenly the old streets grow

Forbidding, haunted, alien,
From Hartford Lane and Sawyer Mill
Up Pepperman to Collier Hill
To Meade, and down through Coglin's Run.

Speaking of Trees

For the tree of the field is man's life.

Deuteronomy 20:19

I'm here with some sugar maples, speaking of trees,
And they're not saying much. In spite of all
The rumors of persistent whispering,
They do not mention genealogies,
Wisdom with all its branches nor the Fall,
As if they wouldn't stand for anything.

We've made them our field representatives,
Rooted in history but branching out,
Replete with trunks, limbs, crowns and sappy hearts,
Sowing their seeds in time, shedding their leaves
In the very autumn Shakespeare writes about,
As if they were our natural counterparts.

They simply do not care, nor break their silence
On our blossoming conceit. And while I hug
Myself against the cool and breezy plain
As the brow of a storm is darkening with violence,
Look how the sugar maples seem to shrug,
Turning their palmate leaves to catch the rain.

Neighboring Storms

Dark clouds are gathering. The trick knee aches.
The hackles itch. She's breezed in drunk again,
Precipitating fears of other men.
Doors slam. A thunderclap of dishes shakes

The wall. And when the storm outside surmounts
Their rain of insults and their muffled threats,
The downpour eavesdrops on their epithets,
The wind delivers blow by blow accounts—

Until it all blows over and sachets
Of honeysuckle scent the morning air.
They chirp like birds, and all is peaceful there.
But me? I'm rattled. I scan the sky for days.

Mister Man of Snow

Ah, Mister Man of Snow,
With your well-versed, wintry mind
And icy, bitumen stare,
You're making your cameo
In a high, supercilious hat
With the unperturbable air
Of the coolest aristocrat
In all of Snowmankind.

You hear no misery
In the sound of the wind nor would
Regard a broken branch
As the limb in a simile,
Set in a cast of light.
Some minor avalanche
May fall from a papery height,
But in general things look good.

Composed by all you see,
You keep a familial watch
Over saw teeth hung from a wire
And beards of snow in a tree.
Pure folly to ask you in
To share a seat by the fire
And weep for women and men
Over a glass of Scotch.

When your arctic continent
Begins to retreat from your ken

And your comrades run from clover,
You will make your wild lament
For all that you had seen,
With your top hat keeling over,
Crying your head off then
On a deepening sea of green.

Up in the Air

Gin-weary, temple on the pane,
I watch the props begin to shake
The sunlight. As we climb, the plane
Trolls its crank bait shadow across a lake.

It drags an airy grappling hook
Over the churches of white towns
Tucked away in the hills that look,
For all their pleated folds, like dressing gowns

Where all the clouds are shaving cream
And powder, periwigs and lace,
The fragments of a lazy dream
That conjures up a ballroom in their place

And finds, across the dreamt parquet,
In a cirrus gown, a girl. Then all
At once this cloying matinee
Dissolves, as if the episodes I call

My life were just such master strokes
Of whimsy, false and protean,
And all I think I love a hoax
Invented by the shadow of a man

Muttering in a windowseat,
Watching a toothless anchor comb
A lake, fooled by his own conceit.
At most, from all of this, someone at home

May shake his head in a reading chair
Or glance up from a gin and lime
At this annoyance in the air,
A minor thing which happens all the time.

Monk's Work

This simple vase merely by being on display
although its dust-dry lip recalls
more storied urns would round
up stars as easily as ferns
keeping them all in order
while keeping them away
shaping the shapeless
atmosphere although
it's made of clay
a potter turned
and turned till
here it turns a
figure of himself
and of that life that
burns to craft of
leaving some-
thing which
will stay
But now I
observe
along
its
blemished glaze the
world bears down with
wilds we can not bear
the wilted ferns and the stars'
oblivion Such a vase might hold
the ash of wasted days but it
does not hold water A crack
appears and gathering
emptiness prepares an
unpropitious face A
monk's work it is
wanting to make
the mundane
be divine
where fearless joy and joyless fear combine
around a baseborn thing I must acknowledge mine

Out here exist
forests of air
dust fall out
darkness to ignite
of a vase and burn away
past a floodlight at
or lint blazing in a
where a minister
the Word or
of meteors which
by lighting up and burning
but around a vase
and a sky of
freshly
These margins
of flights of fancy
of golden
caverns with
or an Appalachian
of straw from a
you are not
The list is endless
unimagined coverts
undreamt Atlantises
than any legend
past all we ever
This is the Region of
where roads in a yellow
where an undiscovered
an unknown range
I didn't know
reside with loves I
Like dust flaring
things come to light
shaping mischievous faces
have to face These
as they stare
it like some

wilds of light
where specks of
of a fertile
around the borders
like snowflakes falling
the corner of a home
stained-glass church
seeks to clarify
like a rain
grant their wish
out Dust to dust of course
the room of ferns
stars appear
arrayed
amass a world
coral reefs jungles
toads and
eyeless fish
barn where a sift
loft alerts you
alone there
and reaches away to
virgin hinterlands
more certainly lost
in the silence
thought to think
There the Land of Not
wood were never noticed
passage leads through
and virtues that
I didn't have
never sought to seek
around these edges
around a central fact
from all that I am not and
too define my vase
right through
vacant place

Taxidermy

An owl hang-gliding in suspended flight,
An arrowheaded fox in mock attack
      Beneath a northern pike
Whose pinking shears are open for a fight
That never comes, a lynx's ears pinned back
      For some decisive strike. . . .

No dove is ever featured in a heap,
No walleye belly up. This art contrives,
      Although the eyes are glass,
To reawaken from their real sleep
Breakneck ferocity when the falcon dives,
      Grace in the largemouth bass,

And overlooks their fixed, affected stare.
A more organic form would represent
      No animal at all,
Its lifetime having melted into air,
But in a fairer attitude present
      An empty pedestal.

Ornamental Motif

Why is it, if you strike an emerald
    A hammer-blow, the gem
Will wear about its crown a diadem
    Of fine, white flour? Why
Do crystals lose their color? Lazuli
    And turquoise ought to craze
To sky blue veins, not cloudy passageways
    Like cobwebbed cracks in glass.
And if white paper, like a looking-glass,
    Reflects all light, a book
Should show your face. But you can't overlook
    That clear rain turns to snow,
A lens will cataract, an undertow
    Of liquid jade will run
Beneath its breaking whitecaps. Williamson,
    Why are you sitting still,
Picturing settings from the windowsill,
    A hand beneath your chin?
The window will become an onionskin.
    Each semiprecious pun,
Each sentimental jewel you fastened on
    Is frangible as glass,
And every crevice is a sheer crevasse.
    That much is crystal clear,
As glaring as the powdered souvenir,
    The crime scene's grisly clue
Of broken spectacles, reminding you
    Of windshields going blind
In starburst faults. Though you are disinclined

To speculate on this,
Even the lives on which you reminisce
Shall fracture like a gem,
The sunlight scattering in all of them.

Three Manuals

I. The Solo Organ

How shall we sing Your song in a strange land?
Dear Lord, why must I answer that today?
      Help me to understand
Your Will. Instruct Your organist to play.

If they don't value someone who can play
Skillfully, then why should I forswear
      To strike a familiar chord,
Collect my check, contribute my métier
      To "Yonder I'll Be There"
And "'Bringing in the Sheaves' with Ernie Ford"?

No long rehearsals. No arguments to bear.
      And Midas on the music board
      Can ululate a hymn
As gay as heard Galuppi's clavichord.
He'll never hear the underlying prayer
That labors after complicated things.
      I brought great music unto them.
      Here's all the good it brings.

One time in high school, as a strategem
      For meeting girls, with whom my flings,
      To date, were none, I joined a band
Referred to by themselves as The G-Strings.
We played one dance, the standard pop a.m.
      I never felt more fraudulent,
Twanging tin sounds and watching an ampersand

Of tissue paper ravel and drift
Through disco lights. Later my father sent
        A note, "Have you returned your Gift?"

        The Cantor at Arnstadt was sent
A letter of complaint, himself, which left
        No doubt that he was too baroque,
        That his accompaniment with "swift
Variations and useless ornament
Confused the congregation and suppressed
        The melody." J.S. Bach
        Left Arnstadt at his own request.

Soli Deo Gloria. Not some ad hoc
        Committee. Lord, if I detest
Bankers and clergymen who watch the clock,
Forgive me. I only seek the blessed phrase
        By which Saul was refreshed,
By which the diapason can amaze.

What voice can reach the sacred organ's praise
        When all the stops are mixed?
Though I may go unheard through all my days,
My heart is fixed, O Lord, my heart is fixed.

II. The Choir Organ

Down at the bank we have a saying,
The customer's always right.
Well, you, me, everybody,
we're the customers.
All I want when I come to church
is a soft pew, a short sermon
and a song I can sing to.
We've had a lot of complaints
that the music on Sunday's too loud.
Now, I don't mind so much
if he wants to shake the bones out of my clothes,
but you can't hear your own voice singing,
which hardly matters
since nobody can sing along anyway.
He's playing Bach and Mozart
and a bunch of guys with names you can't pronounce.
We start off in A or B and next thing you know
he's off in Z-flat major.
Even the choir can't keep up.
They're all looking around
like they lost their car keys.
There's too much practice,
and if they come in late
he's hotter than a scalded dog.
So he's hired a basketful of opera stars.
Every Sunday sounds like "Madame Butterfly,"
and we don't have the money.
Last month he says he wants to buy some more,

a missy soprano and a barreltone.
Well, that dog don't hunt.
I said, "Why don't you spit in one hand
and want in the other
and see which one gets full first?"
He says, "Isn't it worth it
to be proud of our choir?"
I said, "It's not our choir anymore.
It's a band of mercenaries,
a bunch of hired guns.
They might make a joyful racket to the Lord,
but what do they know about us?"

We started Woodbridge Church in 1958
with two dozen people. We wanted a place
to worship with our neighbors
and marry off our kids
and sing our songs.
The first two winters we met in the high school gym
and took turns coming in
at seven to light the furnace,
and still we sat on the bleachers
hunkered down in gloves and overcoats.
Finally we saved enough to buy this land.
The bank did the financing,
and I know for sure that some of those families
were leveraged up to their fillings
just to break ground.
When we were fixing to clear the old barn here
Henry Wilson went up in the loft

And brought down such a cloud of hornets
it looked like he'd been sacking tomcats,
but two days later he was back.
    Later we added the children's wing
and then the Sanctuary next door,
which we're still paying off.
Then we traded in our little bagpipe organ
for this whirlwind from New York,
had to do all kinds of jerryrigging
just to get it in there,
because we wanted the best.
Maybe we're finding out now
that the old one was good enough
for "Amazing Grace" and "The Old Rugged Cross."
The Bible says, Don't be high-minded.
We're regular folks here,
that's the whole idea.
All I'm saying is
give us a regular song.

III. The Great Organ

My name is Cecilia Fairview. Everyone
Has called me Mrs. Fairview for so long
I'm almost startled by my given name.
Back when I was Cecilia, as a girl,
I received instruction in piano
From Mrs. Frank, whose fervor for discipline
May have been masking, as I came to think,
A limited capacity to play.
We lived in a small town in Pennsylvania,
So choices were limited, too. My parents spent
More than they could afford and once a week
Drove across town to my piano lesson,
Usually waiting the hour in the kitchen.
Despite the stern corrections of her ruler,
She loaned me her LPs of Brahms, Chopin
And Handel; and the white dog on the label,
Because my girlfriends all preferred Sinatra,
Would listen in my room with me all night.
In time I became sufficiently proficient
To earn a partial scholarship to college
At Pennsylvania State. Quickly I learned,
However, that what proficiency I had
Derived from patient study, not from talent.
My classmates, some of them, were excellent.
After consistently placing fifth and sixth
In local competitions, I recognized
The youthful dreams I had of musicianship
Would not come true. I finished my degree,

But I had gone as far as I would go.
      Eventually, I married Mr. Fairview,
And we moved here in 1963.
In candor, certain views I have about
God and religion are less than orthodox.
Pressed, I would say I don't believe at all,
But I keep those opinions to myself.
The Church embraced us from the first. My friends
Are here, and I have seen a generation
Of children grow up, marry, and move away,
The four of mine included. For me the Church
has been a way to stay involved in music.
I offer the choir a tolerable soprano,
Accompany on piano now and then,
Usually at rehearsal, and at times
Have even substituted on the organ.
By virtue of my training, I am considered
A sort of expert in that area,
Which isn't really true, but it supplies
A certain status on the music board.

      Mr. Archer in his interview
Did not impress us. Awkward, shy, aloof,
The youngest applicant by far, he seemed
To be concealing his discomfiture
With brusqueness bordering on arrogance.
When asked if we might hear him play, he said,
"You might." And so when he explained that we
Should choose, as he had not prepared a piece,

I selected Widor's difficult toccatta
From "Symphony #5," not only to judge
His touchpiece with another we had heard,
But hoping, I suppose, to see him fail.
        We ventured over to the sanctuary.
I stood behind, above the organ pit,
The others finding seats among the pews.
There was the soft, preliminary thump
Of stops, the gathering expectancy
One always feels before performances,
The weighted, potential energy of waiting.
Then he began. And almost instantly
His virtuoso ease was obvious.
I'm not claiming a "religious experience,"
Or anything like that, don't get me wrong,
But when I looked around the sanctuary
Enriched by Widor's acrobatic flights
I seemed to be seeing it for the first time:
The bands of colored light, the pickled beams
And pews, the curious iconography.
I looked down at the tiny audience,
their passive faces, folded arms, and felt,
just then, I knew some small, important secret,
Such as, I thought, Cecilia once had felt.
        The Church's contract stipulated that
The organist would be evaluated
After one year and, by a majority,
Could be released or permanently hired.
As we awaited Mr. Archer, though,

And Mr. Billingsly was finishing
His plea for "regular songs," we began to hear,
Drifting to our administrative wing,
The sweet, introductory lines of Bach's
"St. Anne," the "Prelude and Fugue in E-Flat Major,"
Which Mr. Archer once explained to me
As "symbolizing Godlike majesty."
Even from our committee room I could
Discern the registers and hear him link
The choir and solo organs to the great,
And I suspected he had picked this piece
In part to show the virtuosity
That manages a triple fugue with grace.
But I could see on the faces of my friends
That they regarded this as a rebuke.
A vote was called, and by a show of hands,
As Mr. Archer led his orchestra
Through one of Bach's most splendid labyrinths,
The organist was formally dismissed.
        My friends walked out into the afternoon
And left, leaving the conference room to me.
I thought about Cecilia, how she watched
That faithful little dog who turned and turned
Around his steady themes, and how she wished
To share those secret passages he knew
With someone close to her, those passages
That lead us far away from little rooms.
I thought a moment of Mrs. Fairview, too.
She had a happy life that might have been

Happier, who can say, but I could see,
If life were scored upon a treble clef,
The onset of a soft diminuendo.
And then I thought of Mr. Archer. He must
Have known he'd lose his post, and I believed
That I could hear all of the counterpoints
He felt: the anger, frustration and resolve
Conjoined with his austere religious faith,
Making the only argument he knew,
The only one he could articulate.
     I wanted him today to compromise
And by a compromise to play the hymns
For everyone, for all my friends, for me.
But he is playing only for himself
And God, and that's a solitary song,
A song that sings itself in a lost valley
And vanishes upon its being heard.
I pictured him alone in the sanctuary
With the high ceiling and the velvet light
Performing for the rows of empty pews,
Striking the keys, pulling out all the stops.

Acknowledgements

Cumberland Poetry Review: "Walter Parmer"

The Formalist: "The Dial Tone," "The Man in the Window," "Story and Song"

The Paris Review: "Up in the Air"

Poet & Critic: "The River Merchant's Wife: A Letter"

Poetry: "The Counterfeiter," "Drawing Hands," "Figures of Speech" (originally "A Picnic in the Park"), "The Mysterious Stranger," "Taxidermy"

Sewanee Review: "Belvedere Marittimo," "Fields of Vision"

The Sewanee Theological Review: "Cross Country," "Outbound," "Smoke Signals," "Annual Returns," "Monk's Work"

Southwest Review: "Eye Strain"

The Tennessee Quarterly: "In the Shield of Athena"

Western Humanities Review: "The Carpenters," "Junkyard"

The Yale Review: "Chant Royal"

I would also like to thank Daniel Anderson, Ellen Barber, Anthony Hecht, John Hollander, John Irwin, Mark Jarman, Philip Stephens, and especially Joseph Harrison and Wyatt Prunty.

Greg Williamson grew up in Nashville, Tennessee. He received degrees from Vanderbilt University, the University of Wisconsin at Madison and The Johns Hopkins University, where he continues as a lecturer in The Writing Seminars. His poems have appeared in *Poetry, The New Republic, Partisan Review, Sewanee Review, The Yale Review, The Paris Review,* and *The New Criterion*.